Campbell

by John Mackay

Lang**Syne**

PUBLISHING

WRITING *to* REMEMBER

LangSyne

PUBLISHING

WRITING *to* REMEMBER

79 Main Street, Newtongrange,
Midlothian EH22 4NA
Tel: 0131 344 0414   Fax: 0845 075 6085
E-mail: info@lang-syne.co.uk
www.langsyneshop.co.uk

Design by Dorothy Meikle
Printed by Ricoh Print Scotland
© Lang Syne Publishers Ltd 2013

ISBN 978-1-85217-036-3

Campbell

SEPT NAMES INCLUDE:

Burnhouse
Burns
Connochie
Denoon
MacConnochie
MacDairmid
MacGibbon
MacIssac
MacKellar
MacKessock
MacOran
MacPhedran
Macure
Ure

Campbell

MOTTO:
Forget not.

CREST:
A Gold Boar's Head.

PLANT BADGE:
Wild myrtle.

TERRITORY:
Argyllshire.

Chapter one:

The origins of the clan system

by Rennie McOwan

The original Scottish clans of the Highlands and the great families of the Lowlands and Borders were gatherings of families, relatives, allies and neighbours for mutual protection against rivals or invaders.

Scotland experienced invasion from the Vikings, the Romans and English armies from the south. The Norman invasion of what is now England also had an influence on land-holding in Scotland. Some of these invaders stayed on and in time became 'Scottish'.

The word clan derives from the Gaelic language term 'clann', meaning children, and it was first used many centuries ago as communities were formed around tribal lands in glens and mountain fastnesses.

The format of clans changed over the centuries, but at its best the chief and his family held the land on behalf of all, like trustees, and the ordinary clansmen and women believed they had a blood relationship with the founder of their clan.

There were two way duties and obligations. An inadequate chief could be deposed and replaced by someone of greater ability.

Clan people had an immense pride in race. Their relationship with the chief was like adult children to a father and they had a real dignity.

The concept of clanship is very old and a more feudal notion of authority gradually crept in.

Pictland, for instance, was divided into seven principalities ruled by feudal leaders who were the strongest and most charismatic leaders of their particular groups.

By the sixth century the 'British' kingdoms of Strathclyde, Lothian and Celtic Dalriada (Argyll) had emerged and Scotland, as one nation, began to take shape in the time of King Kenneth MacAlpin.

Some chiefs claimed descent from

ancient kings which may not have been accurate in every case.

By the twelfth and thirteenth centuries the clans and families were more strongly brought under the central control of Scottish monarchs.

Lands were awarded and administered more and more under royal favour, yet the power of the area clan chiefs was still very great.

The long wars to ensure Scotland's independence against the expansionist ideas of English monarchs extended the influence of some clans and reduced the lands of others.

Those who supported Scotland's greatest king, Robert the Bruce, were awarded the territories of the families who had opposed his claim to the Scottish throne.

In the Scottish Borders country – the notorious Debatable Lands – the great families built up a ferocious reputation for providing warlike men accustomed to raiding into England and occasionally fighting one another.

Chiefs had the power to dispense justice and to confiscate lands and clan warfare produced a society where martial virtues – courage, hardiness, tenacity – were greatly admired.

Gradually the relationship between the clans and the Crown became strained as Scottish monarchs became more orientated to life in the Lowlands and, on occasion, towards England.

The Highland clans spoke a different language, Gaelic, whereas the language of Lowland Scotland and the court was Scots and in more modern times, English.

Highlanders dressed differently, had different customs, and their wild mountain land sometimes seemed almost foreign to people living in the Lowlands.

It must be emphasised that Gaelic culture was very rich and story-telling, poetry, piping, the clarsach (harp) and other music all flourished and were greatly respected.

Highland culture was different from other parts of Scotland but it was not inferior or less sophisticated.

Central Government, whether in London or Edinburgh, sometimes saw the Gaelic clans as

*The spirit of the clan means
much to thousands of people*

a challenge to their authority and some sent expeditions into the Highlands and west to crush the power of the Lords of the Isles.

Nevertheless, when the eighteenth century Jacobite Risings came along the cause of the Stuarts was mainly supported by Highland clans.

The word Jacobite comes from the Latin for James – Jacobus. The Jacobites wanted to restore the exiled Stuarts to the throne of Britain.

The monarchies of Scotland and England became one in 1603 when King James VI of Scotland (1st of England) gained the English throne after Queen Elizabeth died.

The Union of Parliaments of Scotland and England, the Treaty of Union, took place in 1707.

Some Highland clans, of course, and Lowland families opposed the Jacobites and supported the incoming Hanoverians.

After the Jacobite cause finally went down at Culloden in 1746 a kind of ethnic cleansing took place. The power of the chiefs was curtailed. Tartan and the pipes were banned in law.

Many emigrated, some because they

wanted to, some because they were evicted by force. In addition, many Highlanders left for the cities of the south to seek work.

Many of the clan lands became home to sheep and deer shooting estates.

But the warlike traditions of the clans and the great Lowland and Border families lived on, with their descendants fighting bravely for freedom in two world wars.

Remember the men from whence you came, says the Gaelic proverb, and to that could be added the role of many heroic women.

The spirit of the clan, of having roots, whether Highland or Lowland, means much to thousands of people.

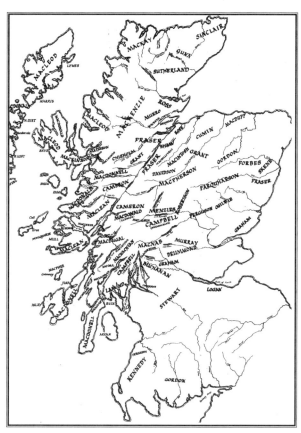

A map of the clans' homelands

Chapter two:

A dynasty is born

The first Campbells were a Scots family who crossed from Ireland to the land of the Picts

The clan Campbell originated from the name O'Duibhne, one of whose chiefs in ancient times was know as Diarmid and the name Campbell was first used in the 1050s in the reign of Malcolm Canmore after a sporran-bearer or purse-bearer to the king previously called Paul O'Duibhne was dubbed with his new surname.

Historians, after such obscure and even

legendary times, have agreed that the clan name comes from the Gaelic 'cam' meaning crooked and 'beul', the mouth, when it was the fashion (as with Malcolm Canmore himself – his 'Canmore' defined in English as 'large head') to be surnamed from some unusual physical feature, in this instance by the characteristic curved or crooked mouth of the family of what is certainly one of the oldest clan names in the Highlands.

It was the Marquis who insisted that he was descended from a Scots family in Ireland who had crossed as emigrants to what was then mostly the land of the Picts to establish the first Scots colony in the district of Dalriada – a comparatively small part of what we know today as Argyll at the heart of what would in time become the kingdom of Scotland. It is marked by the fort at Dunadd, off the A816 a few miles north of Lochgilphead, set in the inlet called Loch Gilp off from Loch Fyne.

So the Campbells began a gradual dominance of the lands of Argyll – north to Loch Awe by the end of the 13th century and becoming allies of Robert the Bruce in his initial efforts to win an independence from the English domination of the southern extent of what had now become the land of the Scots.

Colin Campbell, one of the first of the family of whom we have any definite record, was killed in a fight with another rising clan – the Macdougalls in 1294. His burial place at Kilchrennan Kirk on the north-west shore of Loch Awe is marked by a memorial stone given by the 8th Duke of Argyll.

Colin's son, Sir Neil Campbell of Lochawe, was the man who established the Campbells as a distinctive power in the land.

When the odds were against Robert Bruce, Sir Neil allied himself to that future king of Scots and when Bruce was forced in the early days of the fight for independence to temporarily vanish from the scene it was Neil who helped to arrange a sea crossing to a Western Isles refuge.

As his second wife, Sir Neil married Lady Mary, sister of the now crowned King Robert the

Bruce. From his first marriage, Neil's son Colin also fought for Bruce; and in the gradual process of winning back Scottish strongholds from the English invaders, the castle at Dunoon fell to Colin who was appointed its Constable and later succeeded his father as Sir Colin.

His grandson of the same name was the leader of this branch of the Campbells in Robert III's reign and of his sons Duncan became the first Lord Campbell of Lochawe.

With Royal grants of lands the Campbell estates brought wealth to the family, enabling them to enrich the Church and Abbeys in Scotland. Travels abroad were made by Lord Campbell where he is said to have killed a wild boar in France – commemorated by the animal's head heraldically portrayed on the Campbell arms and badge.

Duncan's son Archibald – 'a man of great spirit and a terror to his enemies' – although said to have died in early manhood, had a son Colin who in time was created 1st Earl of Argyll.

During the minority of this 1st Earl of

Argyll-to-be he was tutored by his uncle Colin of Glenorchy who was the driving force behind the building of the town of Inveraray and the Castle of the same name. Inverarary Castle became the headquarters of the chief of the clan, as it remains today. It should be remembered, however, that as with other noted Highland families, there are often many branches of the family who rule over their particular domains – the Campbells of Balcardine for example.

Colin of Glenorchy would seem, along with his wife Margaret Stewart of Lorn, to have been very energetic improving his estates. And while he was on his travels abroad, Margaret caused the Castle of Kilchurn to rise, dramatically sited at the head of Loch Awe.

Colin, the first Earl, married Isabella Stewart of Lorn and the lands of Lorn became part of the Argyll estate; and from then on the heir to the Earldom was titled Lord Lorne, and later, Marquis of Lorne on future heirs.

The Argyll arms show the galley of Lorn. Also with the marriage the castle near Dollar had its name changed from Gloom Castle to Castle Campbell.

The 2nd Earl of Argyll, Archibald, was made Chancellor of Scotland and at the tragic Battle of Flodden he led the right wing and died alongside his king, James IV, who met a similar fate.

Colin, the 3rd Earl, was made a kind of

Colin, the third Earl, was charged with stamping out lawlessness in the Borders

Overlord of the Scottish Borders by James V and was titled Lieutenant of The Merse, Teviotdale and Lauderdale which entailed efforts to subdue the Douglases – the Borders family who were ever, in the lawless living style, a menace to Royal rule. One of Colin's sisters married a Maclean of Duart who in time planned to get rid of her. Since Maclean chose that she be drowned, apparently since this method meant that he would not need to be present himself at such a foul deed, he employed his henchmen to abduct the lady and take her to a rocky shore where she could be tied to a rock to await the incoming tide.

To this day the act is commemorated at the Lady's Rock off the Isle of Mull on the Firth of Lorne near Duart Castle. One version tells that her long tresses were tied to the tough strands of seaweed spread on the flat upper surface of the rock and she was left to drown. But this barbaric act was foiled for in the Campbells' hunt for the vanished wife news spread that there had been an abduction. She was soon rescued by Campbell followers and returned to safety with the clan.

The wife who was left to die –
until rescued by the Campbells

Chapter three:

Evictions and murder

The Earl's brother, Sir John Campbell, had married the heiress to the Thane of Cawdor. She had grown up with the Campbells for they had stolen her from her family as a baby. The reason is not given. However, Sir John is mentioned in connection with the Lady's Rock incident for, the Campbells swearing reprisals for the abduction by the Macleans, had to 'nurse their wrath to keep it warm' until Sir John had the opportunity to murder Maclean as he lay on his bed during a stay in Edinburgh.

Naturally the Maclean clan in turn swore revenge and this was how one more feud was born between Highland families.

Archibald became the 4th Earl in 1529. He was one of the important members of the Scottish Kirk who inspired the Scottish Reformation.

This 7th Earl co-operated with the

Government of the time to put down the unruly clans not loyal to the Crown – especially in the West Highlands. He did the job so thoroughly that it resulted in him having to dig deep into his funds. The Crown, by way of rewards, presented him with the lands of Kintyre – and asked him to build a new town on the Mull of Kintyre. Thus Campbelltown, named after the family, was duly built.

Colin Roy Campbell of the Red Hair (1708-1751) had, on his father's death, been given the lands of Glenure. He was a farmer and cattle breeder and in 1744 was still unmarried, having not, as yet, as he wrote in a letter 'dipped into love'.

With the Rising of the '45, he joined the Earl of Loudon's regiment and continued in military service until the peace of 1748. As with his elder brother Ian Du, he was appointed a factor on some of the forfeited estates; some of the tenants had been, or were, for the Jacobite cause.

Meantime, Colin had 'dipped into love' and married young Janet Mackay, granddaughter of the 3rd chief of that clan.

Colin was a friend of the leading Stewart

resident in the district under his factorship – 'James Stewart of the Glen' – until trouble rose regarding planned evictions of tenants from several farms. Colin had been accused of favouritism by James Stewart who journeyed to Edinburgh to plead the case of the evicted tenants arguing that they had always paid their rents.

Colin in turn went to Edinburgh where he received Government assurance that the evictions would be carried out. From then, Colin was a target for the opposition.

Enter the 'evil genius' of the whole affair

Anger over Glen evictions

– Allan Breck Stewart. He had been at Culloden and had escaped to France. On his return he stayed near Glenure House with a son of James Stewart and was also a rent collector where he took the opportunity of spreading scandal about Colin of Glenure, saying he had been brutal to the wounded Highlanders at Culloden when in reality Colin had been with his regiment in Aberdeen on other duties.

Colin by this time knew that there were men plotting against him and returning from business in Fort William remarked, as he reached the Ballachulish ferry, 'I am safe, now that I am out of mother's country.' (She was a Cameron of Lochiel.)

The travellers crossed the ferry and in single file set out for Glenure in a road rising among a belt of trees. First the sheriff officer then Colin and his nephew Mungo, both on horses, and a servant with luggage bringing up the rear. Suddenly, a shot echoed across the slopes and Colin of Glenure fell from his mount and died soon afterwards. His nephew ran up the brae from where he guessed the shot had been fired and was just in time to see a man with a gun disappear from sight among the trees.

A few days after the murder, the nephew wrote, 'My aunt has behaved like an angel, no woman ever behaved with greater prudence.'

Janet already had two babies and was pregnant with a third who when the girl was born, was named Colina, after her father.

Who fired the shot that killed Colin of Glenure? This has intrigued historians through the years – and one writer – Robert Louis Stevenson who brought the killing into his novel 'Kidnapped' where the culprit is named as Allan Breck.

The real Allan was suspected but had vanished abroad and Colin's relatives led by Ian Du saw to it that a culprit must be found to avenge the murder. A Stewart? Historians consider that Donald Stewart of Ballachulish was the likeliest to have fired the shot but James Stewart – 'James of the Glen' – was arrested, convicted and hanged.

The trial had been held at Inveraray with William Grant of Prestongrange, the Lord Advocate, chief counsel for the prosecution. The

Duke of Argyll, Lord Justice General, presided so the verdict was automatic.

Archibald, Lord Lorne, the 10th Earl, was made 1st Duke of Argyll by King William I.

The Duke raised a regiment to fight in the Flanders wars and his son was a Colonel at the age of 17. When he succeeded his father in 1703, he was one of the negotiators for the Union of the Parliaments in 1707.

The 3rd Duke together with Duncan Forbes of Culloden formed companies from local volunteers who were dressed in dark tartan and worked for the Government. Their duties included 'containing' the Highlands. These volunteers were nicknamed the Black Watch, a forerunner of the famous regiment.

The Duke died without male issue and was succeeded by Lieut. General John Campbell of Mamore.

The 5th Duke succeeded his father in 1770 and in time became a Field Marshall. He and his Duchess Elizabeth entertained Dr. Johnson and Boswell at Inveraray Castle in 1773.

Chapter four:

More great clansmen

In 1975 fire destroyed part of the Castle and Campbells from all over the world subscribed for its restoration. Once more in summertime, this headquarters of one of the great clans of Scotland, welcomes visitors.

The brother of the 5th Duke, Lord Frederick Campbell, was first Director of the new Register House in Edinburgh. He brought to the Government's attention the sorry state of the country's historical papers and was instrumental in restoring and preserving such important documents.

All three of the following Dukes of Argyll were specialists in the development of agriculture in their lands and of the three, the 8th Duke was Secretary of State in India in the Gladstone government and also a writer who was a friend of Tennyson.

The 8th Duke died in 1900, succeeded by

his son John who married Princess Louise, Queen Victoria's daughter and was Governor General of Canada from 1878 to 1883.

He died in 1914. His nephew Niall Diarmid became the 10th Duke and he was succeeded by a cousin Ian Douglas Campbell.

Apart from the notable Campbells already mentioned, there was Thomas Campbell (1777-1847), Lord Rector of Glasgow University who helped found the University of London.

Duncan Campbell, who was born deaf and dumb but gifted with the 'second sight' and whose father's adventures as a shipwrecked mariner interested Daniel Defoe of 'Crusoe' fame.

Sir Colin Campbell, Lord Clyde, Commander-in-chief during the Indian Mutiny.

The Rt. Hon. Sir Henry Campbell-Bannerman, Prime Minister 1906-8.

And in recent times John Lorne Campbell of Canna, collector of Gaelic songs and folktales, many passed on by oral tradition from Viking times.

Nor should Sir Malcolm Campbell and

his son Donald be forgotten, men of land and water record-breaking speeds.

Of the chieftains, the 15th is Sir Niall Alexander Campbell, Hereditary Keeper of Balcardine Castle.

Today's chief of all the Campbells – the 26th, is the 12th Duke of Argyll, Sir Ian Campbell, Keeper of the Great Seal of Scotland, and of the Castles of Dunoon, Carrick, Dunstaffnage and Tarbert; and Admiral of the Western Coast.

A Campbell chief honours one of his men

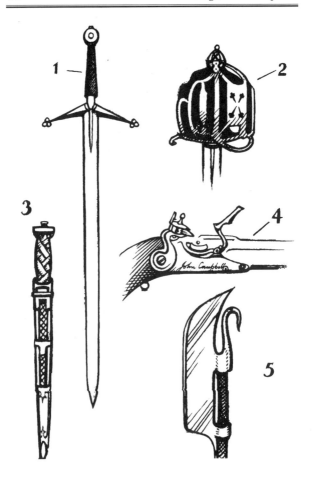

Highland weapons

1) The claymore or two-handed sword
   (fifteenth or early sixteenth century)

2) Basket hilt of broadsword
   made in Stirling, 1716

3) Highland dirk
   (eighteenth century)

4) Steel pistol *(detail)* made in Doune

5) Head of Lochaber Axe as carried
   in the '45 and earlier